Peccadilloes

Peccadilloes

Jan Schreiber

White Violet Press

ISBN-13:978-0615915241

White Violet Press
24600 Mountain Avenue/35
Hemet, California 92544

Contents

Brief Lives

The Road to Nowhere	11
Closing Time at the Freedom Lounge in Vassalboro	13
The Grifter at Heaven's Gate	14
For Someone	16
La Vespa	17
Wisconsin	18
It's July and It Will Always Be July	19
The Reverend Charles Colby	20
The Pianist	21

Sonnets on Various Occasions

The Aging Lover Flies into the Night	25
The Stone Mason	26
Song of the Golden Bowl	27
Lament of the Maker	28
The Inventory	29
A Man of the World Contemplates Heaven	30
Report of the Committee	31

Album

The Wastebasket	35
Command Performance	36
A Little Night Music	37
Dots	38

The Level Crossing   39

Notes from the Party   41

Lost in the Sculpture Garden   42

February Fantasy   43

Prophecy   44

A Brief Dangerous Moment   45

Orvieto   47

Digression on a Theme   49

Adam and the Animals   50

Seasonal Summary   51

Short Takes

Hardy Perennial   55

In Praise of Cognitive Silence   56

Your Idea of Heaven   57

What's Hard for a Man   58

Five-finger Exercise   59

Spider   60

One Crow Sorrow   61

The Bottom Line   62

The Angler   63

A Man Is But a Fleeting Flower   64

All Politics Is Tense   65

The Hedge   66

Voice at the End of the Line   67

The Crowd   68

A Change of Heart   69

Beach Glass

Penobscot Bay	73
What's Left	75
Night Piece for Anna	76
Naked on the Island	77
Cormorants	78
Musseling	79
Near Sunset	82

For Frances

Brief Lives

The Road to Nowhere

No one knew why he built
a road over a mountain.
It started close to home
and wound through trees, past cliffs
not visited in years,
bound for the sea, but stopped
before it got there, somewhere
halfway down a hill.

They said, why build a road
that goes nowhere? But
it goes somewhere. It goes
out to a rocky shelf
that overlooks the steady
unceasing breakers far
below the traveler
who moves while standing still.

Perhaps if it were finished –
but it will never be
finished. It runs toward
not to the sea, an arc,
a proposition in
geometry, a brief
infinity of points
along a finite line.

It was for him a mode
of recall, of the son
who loved this place and years
ago despairing or
in madness killed himself.
Walking the road, he saw

what could not be left out
in the many tellings.

It made a kind of solace.
Yielding to rocks and shadows
at the end of order,
he waited for the long
susurrus in the trees
brushing across the land
like half-formed memory
or like the coming rain.

Closing Time at the Freedom Lounge in Vassalboro

It's not that bad tonight.
Scoop was too drunk to fight.
Sox lost. Nomar's got heart.
Guy owes me rent paid part.
Buddy dropped by to say
his daughter's due in May.
I haven't heard from mine
in eight years – but I'm fine.
Still on the haul. The days
get longer. Got a ways
to go to clear this debt.
It'll take years of sweat.

I'm on the highway. Wide
rigs close on either side.
We're racing past this town.
It's too late to slow down.
The squeal, the crash, the flame
spreading across the frame,
then white heat everywhere.
And you can only stare
into this hell and see
the beauty of the burning:
my flesh and fury turning
to ash and breaking free.

The Grifter at Heaven's Gate

After some decades I got used to lying
to them about myself, to me about
how much I'd take before I threw them out.
I also lied about my fear of dying.

In age we finally celebrate success
in mastering that most pliable invention:
the self through which we have no faint intention
of letting others see the soul's distress.

And once the mask is fixed, the rest will follow –
the symbols of control that we and they
are taken in by, or the balls to say
loss doesn't matter – but that's pretty hollow.

I've been with more than one who talked that way
until the full force hit them, then they caved.
At times I wonder if I could have saved
them from the ravages of clarity.

Not that I'm trying to sound unduly tough.
There isn't much to gain in piling on
to make a jackass of some sorry son
who takes it hard when someone calls his bluff.

So now that I am picking up my winnings
it's time at last to set the record straight –
and in a way you can appreciate
because you know there won't be extra innings.

I played the parts, aware what I was paying.
I fished for easy praise but knew the score,
and lost but still kept coming back for more.
I saw the outcome but I kept delaying.

The kids who follow me will do the same:
cock-sure and ready, tensed up for the fight.
Breathing aromas of a summer night,
they play before they understand the game.

And now I'm checking out, we're almost even.
I got some satisfaction for my bit,
although it's true I never made a hit,
but left some of my blood there on the pavement.

You'll see it if you care to have a look.
And someone searching in some far-off season
might sense a meaning or infer a reason –
but that's not very likely. Close the book.

For Someone

On the bright wall shadows
of leaves stir and recall
the erotic afternoon.
All our lives are fleeting
precision. You most of all
yesterday were vivid.

La Vespa

Poised on a blade
of grass, knife edge,
she flies off at
the slightest touch.

Devious but
firm of intent,
she can ride out
the rain and wind.

She fears attack,
distrusts allure;
but a mere look
feeds her desire.

With numberless
eyes for the world's
green openness,
she seeks new fields.

Bright colors sparkle
from her wing.
Many are crippled
by her sting.

Wisconsin

Earlier, through stones and burdock and under
barbed wire, the dog had raced each August day
out to the fields of timothy and beyond
to where the Guernseys, swollen with the glut
of summer, grazed beneath mountains of cloud.
Darting and feinting, she brought in the herd
past the long shadows of the row of trees,
the maples and box elders and forked birch,
granite picked from the fields lining their ranks,
and through the muddy barnyard, each to her stall
to wait for callused hands to pull the teats,
relief as the milk sang in the galvanized pail.

But now with snow lying waist-deep in the barnyard,
life is defined by the narrow paths a man
can shovel. The dog trots out to the pump and sniffs
cold iron against the acrid moist manure
smell of the barn. Pitchforks and rubber boots.
The steamy breath of cows. The temperature
for weeks not topping zero. Each day he breaks
ice from the trough, hefts feed sacks, splits stove wood.
In the long solitary hours a man
inclined to thought ranges the world and sighs,
imagining a calling, what one does
with leisure, tended lawns, and books at hand;
feeling here in winter's dusk that pleasure
is meager as heat. But who would guess his heart
when, back on the porch, the barn chores done, he gazes
out at the night to see, eerie and transient
as wordless longing, the pale blue northern lights?

It's July and It Will Always Be July

A boat against the dock,
flared gunwale and ribbed flooring,
old motor at the back,
trances a boy who's pouring
gas and oil, spilling
a rainbow on the water.
The dog, his short tail flailing,
bounds into the three-seater.

An old man dozing in
a lawn chair doesn't hear
the women making plans
or see the rotting pier,
yet waking, senses, lodged
like song, the engines' whine,
and past the outmost edge
of sight, the strake's curved line.

The Reverend Charles Colby

Baptist, sent two sons to Harvard, then
that fateful day in 1922
learned that his wife had died in surgery.
Hours later, sitting down to dinner with
her mother and his daughter, twelve, he raised
his reddened eyes above their heads to say
"We will not ask the blessing here today."

Next day he bought a puppy for the girl
but, baffled in his grief at bringing up
a wounded adolescent female child,
sent her to live with her no-nonsense aunt
who had a daughter of her own and knew,
he thought, where women go at times like these
to purchase feminine necessities.

She loved him still and, grown or nearly so,
followed him out to California where
in the Depression he sold Bibles and
his second wife raised chickens to sustain them.
It stirred his heart to see the girl begin
her college years with all he had to give:
principles and the fierceness to maintain them.

Back to Wisconsin, where he'd finally got
a parish. Out behind the parsonage
deer stripped the apple trees. She took the train.
He met her at the station holding ice cream.
That fall he saw her married, then set off
into the woods with tent and fishing rod
to contemplate the mazy grace of God.

The Pianist

Far from all cities, in a harbor town
where unnamed streets meander, dip and turn
down past the lakefront, under sun and cloud
children ride bikes along the puddly road.
Men in short pants and sandals lick ice cream
while strolling toward the park. Another storm
is on the way. Inside the low stone house
the storekeeper's wife is sewing a summer dress,
while on a record Dinu Lipatti plays
sonatas and chromatic fantasies.

She feels her soul expand into a calm
and urgencies that troubled her become
light to the touch, as fingers on the keys
repeat a dissonance until it stays
bound to the theme. Why this vague sense of loss
amid such plenty? Her agile hands retrace
the notes' complexities. It has not left her.
The theme comes round again, but in a softer
guise, as from her piano by the window.
She threads a needle. Later, after sundown,
here in this room she'll summon her response
and play to an enchanted audience.

Sonnets on Various Occasions

The Aging Lover Flies into the Night

From seven miles high, through wispy vapor
I can see rivers: narrow silver ribbons
that start beyond vision, turn and wind forever,
catching the sun and running with it into
the undefined. Imponderable body whose lines
speak your geology – of glaciers, old
upheavals, rain. How have those snaky veins
enticed your parts together till they lulled
me with their bounty in the fading light!
How flat their waves and rapids from this height,
how motionless the currents that give pulse
and mystery to your skin! With the mind's hand
I trace your devious contours as we race
from reverie down corridors of stone.

The Stone Mason

He builds from local rocks that come to hand –
craggy, irregular, or water-worn –
and guided by a form he has in mind
but nothing like a plan, nothing so stern.

Colors and sizes join haphazardly
except for some that draw themselves together;
some likely stones he has to throw away,
a few so small they are not worth the bother.

And gradually the thing materializes,
assumes the shape he'd say he worked to build
although the details harbor some surprises
and there are places where he'd say he failed.

A century from now all will be changed
except the pile of rocks that he arranged.

Song of the Golden Bowl

In what imaginary galaxy
are they assembled – rare and passing gifts
of earth, broken or crushed or burnt to ash?

And to what hell in time are they consigned –
the instants when in rage or carelessness
someone destroyed a lovely, hard-won thing?

The mind's desire has no ecology.
Some losses no new pleasures can revoke.
Yes, art is long, destruction brief; its flash
reduces years of thought and pain to smoke.

Today's enchantment is tomorrow's dust.
Luck hovers at the artisan's quick hand
and luck protects the work – or failing just
an eyelid's blink, sees glass revert to sand.

Lament of the Maker

What wonders I've performed, with leaping mind,
imagining the fruit while eyeing the seed,
conjuring what's ahead while still behind,
savoring praises for the undone deed.

I have esteemed my skill so highly that
I stroll through mansions I have yet to build
and, like the seigneur or the plutocrat,
reap harvests from rich fields I have not tilled.

But when I face the drudgery of art,
bright mirrors where misunderstandings lurk,
my faltering strength just when the need is great,
I faint before the task – or rashly start,
push through to make an end, survey my work,
and smile – how fine, how small, how light in weight!

The Inventory

She held me in her arms, cradled my head
against her breast, and in love's dotage fell
to tallying gray hairs, my belly's spread,
the stains of age and weather that foretell
decrepitude, my crooked back and knee ...
Were I a soldier from the battlefield
and she a nurse, would she relentlessly
thus catalog my scars while I lie peeled
beneath her gaze?
                Oh, show some pity, Love,
and if you have it in you, summon up
that buoyancy in face of mortal pain
that comforts cowards and makes heroes of
strong women. When you hoist my meager cup,
feign pleasure in the spirits that remain.

A Man of the World Contemplates Heaven

From my dim room I see a balcony
covered with vines that filter sun and air.
And there's a table with a waiting chair
facing the snow-capped mountains and the sea.

Bird songs are sounding from a nearby grove
where orange trees blossom, scenting the light breeze.
The balcony invites me, when I please,
into a sensuous aerie fit for Jove.

But something holds me back, so near the door.
Perhaps the view's not all that I assume.
Perhaps the wind's too sharp, the sun too bright ...
This is contentment I can settle for:
always to wait here in my sheltered room,
always a breath away from my delight.

Report of the Committee

We do not have definitive instructions
for inferring the soul from evidence
detected on the skin, the brow, or in
those much-dissembling eyes – the common guise
many have learned to wear. We do not think
even the wise can lay the spirit bare.

What would it mean to understand the whole?
To know its past, foretell the waste and slight
precipitate of time such persons might
amass with just enough indulgence from
the unwary state?
     Better to stop him now,
or else if we allow his days to run,
he may pursue his work without renown
until one day he burns the city down.

Album

The Wastebasket

It's done, for now – the grief,
isolation, rage, despair,
self-hate. The room is small
once more, with just a chair
and couch. The hours have ended.
Leaving their words that loomed
thick in the air, the patients
take up their lives, consumed
again in the unscripted
moment, while the one
who heard their dreadful secrets
and sat with each in the un-
fathomable room
empties the basket's store
of dried tears, rights an errant
cushion, and shuts the door.

Command Performance

Late winter. In a small roadside café
a dozen friends have gathered as they do
each Saturday. Hot soup and sandwiches,
small talk and jokes. Outside, a steady snow
that looks as if it could go on forever.
One tells of meeting Moses Soyer while
teaching a first-year class. One talks about
research on memory. He has a dark
surgical wound along his scalp. He plans
to get a dog. Across from him, his wife
hears with a watchful smile. They learned last week
it was a tumor and he has a year,
give or take. They are in their seventies.

It seemed that there should be no end to this:
Order a simple lunch, talk art, lament
politics, gossip. Every week should be
just like the one before. That's how it was
when they were young, and similar encounters,
rife with their energies and rivalries,
went on for years – or so it seems today.
Went on at least till someone got an offer
you just cannot refuse, and moved away.

A Little Night Music

In Boston's Top-of-the-Hub restaurant with a view of the airport

High over city lights
waiters hasten to wait
on diners driven to sate
a week of appetites.

Paté, poached salmon, wines,
coffee, a mousse: repast
and love.
        But see – out past
fingers enlaced like vines

that artfully encroach –
the distant heavy planes,
lights cutting through light rains,
are making their approach.

Unhurried, they begin
a stately ritual mating
dance, and drawn to earth's waiting
lap, they settle in.

Lovers who woo aloft
eventually descend,
hoping that in the end
their plunge will be as soft.

Dots

Late morning: someone wakes
from restless sleep and finds
her head still aches.

A man unknown to her
berates his lack of spine,
his *trop de coeur*.

A potter at whose place
each separately bought
a lamp, a vase

draws from a red-hot pit
of sand a finely wrought
bowl, rotates it,

and watches colors dance.
Had he observed the grackle
near the fence

he'd think that sheen had caught
the feathers of its neck.
But he had not.

The Level Crossing

At the level crossing the parade
the crowd the traffic and the streetcar all
come together with the sun emerging
just as it should to celebrate the moment –
which is the moment when our expectations
are highest and the long midsummer day
has not yet grown beyond the keyed-up pleasure
in waiting – for the kids at least
                                        But why
else did you come here then? You must have known
it was a level crossing where things jam up
where accidents happen where you can't just go
whenever you get the urge to leave you're so
impatient
                    Listen in the distance a band
is playing you almost can't hear it against
the traffic and the noise the kids are making
the sun is ricocheting off the hoods
of cars dogs are chasing each other through
the crowds young girls tattooed in sunglasses
and skimpy tops are strutting down the sidewalk
people are waving flags and pushing strollers
or eating pizza sipping beer
                                        I think
of all the things I could be doing it's not
as if I'm blessed with all this leisure time

Just then the veterans come by in jeeps
apparently the start of the parade
some people in the crowd are clapping but
we can't see any floats – and down the block
an old guy in the crowd falls to the ground
some people say he had a heart attack

or maybe he just fainted they make a kind
of circle there around him and we see
an ambulance that must have been here all
along move up to where he fell it takes
a long time like a movie in slow motion
but they finally get him loaded and
drive off
        After that the rest of the
parade is kind of anticlimactic the band
is out of key and lacks trombones a woman
near us says it was a heart attack
or so she heard she heard he didn't make it
it wasn't anyone we knew we don't
say anything to the kids they're eating ice cream
now still full of energy still eager
to join in anything
          But we are tired
and start to round them up it's been a long
day and my temper's wearing thin – so maybe
not everyone would read the scene this way
I see some old guys standing by the curb
not all but unmistakably some – waiting
calm amid the celebration waiting
with patience and no protest simply waiting
to get out

Notes from the Party

Bright summer day. The languid, spacious lawn
slopes from the gardens past the breakfast room.
No gifts. The bride is sixty-two. The groom,
that avid sailor, finds some vigor gone
after the radiation. Someone plays
airs on the violin. A young child now
pulls at his mother's hand. *Amazing how
much he resembles you!* A well turned phrase:
He's hers and not, out of a surrogate
by her own husband's sperm – who years before
this marriage, in his thirties, was a more
impassioned lover of the delicate
woman paying the artful compliment –
whose fiancé in turn the radiant bride
had once seduced.
              Thus did love's dice decide,
rolling and tumbling, who was finally meant
for whom. And now in these more steady times
all welcome the patina years have laid
over old feelings. Gracious, calm, arrayed
in casual elegance, each pantomimes
the honored, ancient roles. Delighted, they
all watch the senior psychoanalyst
dance like a dervish with the bride. He'd kissed
her too, years back, hoping fond youth would stay.

Lost in the Sculpture Garden

With smiles askew under stone brows,
ears to the ground, great heads carouse
discreet among the cognoscenti.
Meanwhile the devious innocent
elude their elders, plunge
down hillsides to explore
and wander through the trees
where unhewn boulders graze
along the piney floor.

They taste before they must depart –
Hansel and Gretel caught by artful
layers of desire and seeming.
How soon the young delight in dreaming!
Whatever they were taught,
they've seen a boulder can
morph in a moment, raise
its head and sniff the breeze
as sheep, werewolf, or man.

Tracing the trail out of the pines
back to predictable designs,
they walk as if they now are wiser,
suspicious of protective lies, or
newly untamable
and ready to deceive
the gray world as they try
the sage fruit hoarded by
some prepubescent Eve.

February Fantasy

Rain comes
even in
the depth of winter.

Recall
evenings
when heat still lingered

well past
the final fall
of dark? No heat now.

Almost
in a trance
of flight we follow

the fine
rain's stippled
subtle reflection

as if
all our old
summers were fiction.

Prophecy

Somewhere at this moment
a woman with a bad
diagnosis holds out
against her body's treason.
Her family holds out
little hope against long
odds. Against expectations
spring makes a shy appearance.

Outside, the wind is raw.
Against the warming pane
a lilac branch sprouts leaves
while twigs exposed to sleet
hold back. But not for long:
fast or slow, cells divide
and, multiplying, force
the pale veins down and in.

It will come with all
the urgency of desire
to those who do not desire.
It will not be held back –
this willy-nilly fierce
unwelcome spring, whose servants
shudder with the advent
of each finality.

A Brief Dangerous Moment*

Let's start again from the top.
I enter on the third
beat; you have to keep
the bass line firm. It's hard

to hear the lute against
the harpsichord, and I
know I must have winced:
the light was in my eye.

Yes, I agree the light
is very strong today.
Your earring pearl pops out.
Mine too? Our souls must be

aligned. And Peter's chair
glows like the blacksmith's forge.
It's odd we're so aware
of light. Eyes must take charge

when music stops. I feel
we're standing outside time,
watching a carousel
to see if it will come

alive again, or else
we're lost for eternity.
That's silly – feel my pulse:
firm as the clock. And we,

*Imagined from Vermeer's "The Concert," stolen from the Isabella Stewart
  Gardner Museum (Boston) in 1990 and not recovered.

so solid and so full
of life, won't turn to dust.
For each created soul,
the preachers say, must last.

Surely we'll congregate
in some form centuries
from now, and will you yet
be playing those heartwood keys?

Let's start again from the top.

Orvieto

While she is coaxing poppies to life in paint,
motionless from his rock he scans the valley,
assembling in his mind the words for green –
olive and *emerald, sea foam, chartreuse, plain grass* –
naming the planes of vision in the dusk,
translucent, filtered by the Italian air,

and with an amateur's ingenuous air,
gazes out raptly, watching the sunset paint
the Tuscan scrims descending through the dusk
into the misty reaches where the valley
loses distinction and confuses grass
with gray stone that might harbor a tinge of green.

The distant stucco walls, fragile as green-
ware, peopled by still more fragile, temporary
tenants of this generation, grass
underfoot, seem daubs of ochre paint
an ancient artist laid into the valley
to jolt a scene to life and pierce the dusk

now deepening breath by breath. The years are dusk
scarcely envisioned in the matinal green
when churchmen founded high above the valley
a monastery for a fictive heir.
Now it commands the hill, opaque as paint
running down silk and seeping into grass.

And blade by blade, the cool haphazard grass
recedes into a multilayered dusk,
deepened by memory or alloyed by paint,
while cars winding up roads cut in the green-
blue hillsides throw exhaust into the air
that rises like flawed incense from the valley

and washes out over a neighbor valley
carrying cock-crows and a scent of grass.
Through the far sounds of motors on the air
the present calls the painter from the dusk,
turns her attention from viridian green
that sets off timeless poppies made of paint.

Dark, having closed the valley, perfected dusk,
canceled the layered grass and stolen its green,
leaves relic words in air and dreams in paint.

Digression on a Theme

Un feu distinct m'habite . . .
      – Paul Valéry

What's here is not a flame; more like a voice
that briefly speaks, then fades to nothingness,
leaving enigmas no one can reduce.

Or if it's not a voice, then just an urge
to shape the shifting world that looms so large
and imprecise on vision's ragged edge.

Not even an urge in that too-frequent time
when all you seek is just a quiet room
in which to escape the fast, persistent stream …

But only ticks of seconds passing and
fog lifting for a glimpse, then settling in,
then by the grace of chance lifting again.

Adam and the Animals

How did he know what he had to know to name them?
To call them not with names uniquely theirs
but common words, as if one sound could tame them?

It seems he trusted that if something bears
a word, its fellow will show up again
someday, to catch a speaker unawares

and prove a likeness. Things have *thingness* when
they may recur unbid to mind or sight
and call their labels forth from other men.

But he was wild, untutored, penny-bright
and new to tongue. How many suns rose high
in all those skies before he saw the light

and gave them sudden being: "sun" and "sky"?
He started with the wonders he could see.
Some late descendant, blocked and wondering why,

looked inward, found "desire," "perplexity" –
feelings that swirled until they were defined.
Ur-diagnostician, did you guess that we

would turn your swift surmises into mind?

Seasonal Summary

Out of that thick-walled, chipped ceramic mug
    that holds a morning glory vine
you'd hoped to paint, to catch the twisting buds
    in potency, frozen in time,

this morning two improbable blue flames
    hurled fanfares toward the window light
with the last life their severed stems retained
    from summer rains and radiant skies.

The petals of those virgin blooms are smooth
    as new desire made palpable.
Outside, October's grass is coated with
    the adamant hoarfrost of fall.

With earth's mechanic swing, the ungrounded flowers
    follow the arc and fade of light
as a condemned man counts diminished hours
    while his vast riches dissipate.

Short Takes

Hardy Perennial

Death stopped the fiery energy
with which the sun infused the tree,
leaving the log that flames consume
to heat the humble living room
where an optimistic man and wife
couch to conceive another life.

In Praise of Cognitive Silence

The circuits close, bright comebacks come
quick to his mental maps.
Pity the man who can't keep mum
after the synapse snaps.

Your Idea of Heaven

The people have profound and thought-worn faces.
They all have lived in cosmopolitan places,
pursuing life at superhuman paces.
In art and science they have led the way.
Wisdom shines forth in everything they say,
and none of them give you the time of day.

's Hard for a Man

To examine what he knows
and say with certainty
if his conviction rose
from something he could see,

was told, thought likely, or
most wanted to be true.
Caution depletes the store
of facts, and thins the stew

of speech to gentle tea
flavored with common sense
where men dip gingerly
crumbs of experience.

Five-finger Exercise

Zeno, I pray
your arrow finds
its mark someday
but not while I've
come just halfway.

Spider

Defier of Nature's iron law,
flouter of gravity, you impinge
on the blank, barren places, flaw
in our emptiness, arachninja!
Until at last the upper-bound
surface of your vast surround –
this ceiling, proof against debris,
assaulted by your cables hurled
between the walls and purity –
falls to the real, corrupted world.

One Crow Sorrow

yellow chair
foggy air
at the landing
sit and stare

engines shake
widening wake
regret explain
excuse forsake

gulls wheel low
and the crow
you had your moment
let it go

The Bottom Line

Reduce exposure, and in time
your sinking fortunes start to climb.
Therefore take heart: beyond a doubt
with bottom in, you'll bottom out.

The Angler

Pompous has found a worthy mark at last:
young and amazed, she dotes upon his airs,
swallowing lines he's practiced years to cast.
She strikes, he reels, as they go up the stairs.

A Man Is But a Fleeting Flower

She'd always craved a single perfect rose
but no one form embodies all perfection,
so she embraced the dozens that came close
and knew her heart's ideal by indirection.

All Politics Is Tense

The future tense can be your friend:
promise – the crowd's delighted.
The past tense holds your fate in hand:
deny – and you're indicted.

The Hedge

We talk across the hedge.
Death leans and smokes
like an old friend
with whom one jokes …
but always there's an edge.

Voice at the End of the Line

Attention, all who stride or stand:
The moving walkway is nearing its end.

The Crowd

They watched him drawn and quartered,
    the wretched sinner,
and when they got back home
    sat down to dinner.

A Change of Heart

She always said the smart ones were depressed
and that her husband didn't pass the test.
It wasn't till he died that she felt doubt,
surprised he had the brains to blow them out.

Beach Glass

Penobscot Bay

On deep blue sun-
spangled water bob strewn
dots of white, vermillion,
orange and green –
the gay displays
of lobster buoys.
Profuse illusion
greets those who brave
the implacable sun.

Calypso bless
this cloudless day,
this stark unconsummated blue …
Listen: over far plains fabled
horses are flinging
shuddering hooves, and through
the star-pierced night
a man and wife are driving, singing
to stay awake, their disabled
child asleep in the back seat.

But fear, I said, is an isotope of
pleasure. It has to be, he said, because
we cannot unalloy.
The prow meets waves
oblique, oblivious.
Bright markers full of promise dance,
nod and retreat. Still longing late
on a beam reach,
we reach a veiled reconnaissance
with the wandering, surf-charmed boy.

Someone is painting this scene, using
only primary colors and thus
falsifying, you must agree,
a never-seen immensity
unconveyable by light
and shadow, salt and sound.
Yet happiness, he said, is not delight,
nor ecstasy nor triumph, but a calm
acceptance, unrefusing.
Then why is it recalled, foreseen,
but never found?

Only the chop
and rush below
are constant.... Here,
you take the wheel. Steer
for the island dead ahead.
Time is mere
motion. Yes
but you cannot stop
it. You cannot.
Stop.

Caught in the winds of memory,
deflected from the course,
look to the weather.
It focuses the swell.
The small bird whistles homeward
and the nimble gull
hangs on the current.
Out of these watery syllables
the day begins to gather force
and through the hull
I feel the icy revelations tremble.

What's Left

When my keen fury fades
and time has blurred these eyes,
after your grief subsides
and tactile memory goes,
can you recapture me?
Each year in a private hour
visit the rock-edged sea
where winds across the shore
blow as they used to blow
and in the rhythmic swell
you hear old poems. Now
see what you can recall
from our brief years that still
beat like a wave-struck bell.

Night Piece for Anna

Still in the waning light
as orange clouds marbleize
what was a silver sky
and pines at water's edge
darken to silhouette,
still are you leaning there
to capture with your brush
the nuances of glowing
alive yet to your eye.

Below you on the ledge,
warmth fading from the air,
the old cat stares at dusk
watching the dark shapes massing.

What spirit aids the unknowing
witnesses of the storm,
helpless against all harm,
whose alert eyes still trap
the fading light and keep
watch and do not weep
their short day's passing?

Naked on the Island

Peace in the house, and in
the distance a high wind.
Move in the web of memory,
neither bound nor free,
hearing the foghorn and
an underlying sound.
Beyond the porch, rock.
Beyond the rock, water.
Beyond the water, water.
Water and the void
beyond the rock, beyond
water, beyond words.
Surely it won't be long.
Touch hands, lie still, listen
to the rise and fall of breaths
racing through the night.

Cormorants

Black and sleek as steely-eyed
deacons, ascetic and aloof,
      the cormorants
disdain the jostling waves, riding
peaks and troughs, placid as flatirons.
      One suddenly
upends and disappears a full
minute or more, some fifty yards
      away emerging.
Preying and gorging, they float fastidious,
always unruffled, unperturbed
      by appetite.

Though half-submerged they do aspire.
Persuaded finally into flight
      they gather speed
and skip tiptoe on wave tips like
flat stones flung side-arm from the shore,
      wings flailing.
Full bellies when they would be light
belie the anorexic pose,
      rob them of grace.
With difficulty they enter heaven,
rise and take dominion, running
      unopposed.

Musseling

Through the causeway sluice
the sea pours with the tide.
In rubber thongs I brace
myself for cold and wade
into the shallows on
up-ended blue-black shells
of mussels. As I lean
over their draining pools
they're savoring the current
through parted beaks. Jammed tight,
barnacle-crusted, ancient
as time, half-calcified:
an underwater lea
endlessly spreading. In knots
of rock and fiber, they
remain immobile, bits
of armored flesh with habits
of plants. I've long been waiting
to pick these flowers, snippets
of sea life for a floating
basket.
       But those who dine
on what the oceans yield
have learned a fine disdain.
And knowing that these wild
mussels are slight of flesh
I search the crowded beds
for prizes. In the crush
of shells and stones the odds
of great gain while the tide
permits are small – and yet
one hopes. And so I load
the basket weight by weight,

taking what vision, reach
and chance bring to my hand.
In this attentive crouch
I scavenge in no end
of plenty with the gong
of bell buoys in my ears.
I have been scavenging
in truth down all these years,
with worry at my back
waiting for the random
hand at last to pluck
me from the salty garden
where I've grown old and sipped
a fraction of the vast
surrounding sea.
              So rapt
in sea dreams I'm possessed
by rhythms of waves and feel
in ebb and flow of blood
and air a tidal pull
straining the old divide.

Entranced, I might have drowned,
and willingly, for shadow
shimmering just beyond
the surface beckons, widens,
promises. Instead
I wake to wariness
and take up what I've made
a substitute for loss.

Though I'm not done, it's time
to leave these timeless pools
where, bent and intent, I've roamed
gathering onyx shells.

Regaining a land-bearing,
I make my way to shore
and like a laggard day-
dreaming schoolboy, hearing
the bell and dimly aware,
head home the longer way.

Near Sunset

Now it's full summer and the air's alive.
We're driving over winding island roads,
depleted by a tense and strenuous day.
Preoccupied, we mull the lawsuit and
the long estrangement of our fragile child.
Uncertainty and worry dim the scene.
Each of us has learned a role to play:
resilient, proud, good-humored in the face
of disappointment. I am slow to admit
how hard it has become to seem so steady.

Ahead of us we see a yellow truck
and in the back a clutch of teens are waving,
leaning out as the driver rounds a bend.
We can't get close enough to make out faces.
Sometimes they disappear and we're alone
amid the rocks and darkening trees, the cool
blue shadows blanketing the spaces. Then
the spooling road straightens again and there
they burst in view, still leaning, waving like
a circus troupe to draw the stragglers in.
Among the carney folks it's called a tease –
something to pique the interest or allure
the casual stroller, ease him toward the main
attraction. But I think these kids have no
such aim. A summer evening, no regrets
or obligations. Being alive is all.

"I'd like to be like that," I say aloud.
And once on open ocean, all alone,
I looked for shore as fog rose in the east
and saw no solid for the mind to seize,
and all the world a path and therefore none.

But here is road sufficient to forget
as we, complicit, ride the summer breeze
till we become the yellow truck, the piper
clad in motley, dancing on ahead
to music made of shimmering island air,
the distant voice of coves, the swaying trees
marking the random path through pathless woods,
with laughter like the loons across the water,
beneath the woven boughs that verge the water,
drawing us to the sun, still drawing us
to years we left behind and hope to know
at last for what they really were – until
the road runs out and there is only sun …

Acknowledgments

The author thanks the following magazines, in which many of the poems in this collection first appeared, for permission to reprint: *Christian Science Monitor, Edge City Review, Expansive Poetry & Music, The Formalist, Iambs & Trochees, Not Just Air, Pivot, Plains Poetry Journal, Raintown Review.*

Jan Schreiber has published three previous books of poems: *Digressions*, *Wily Apparitions*, and *Bell Buoys*. He has also published two books of translations – *A Stroke upon the Sea* and *Sketch of a Serpent* – and a collection of critical essays called *Sparring with the Sun*. He lives in Brookline, Massachusetts.